THE TRUTH
ABOUT
MENTAL
TELEPATHY

THE TRUTH ABOUT

AN ESSANDESS SPECIAL EDITION • NEW YORK

MENTAL
TELEPATHY

BETH BROWN

To Bea Moore
for wisdom of the heart

THE TRUTH ABOUT MENTAL TELEPATHY
SBN: 671-10534-5
Printed in the U.S.A.
Designed by Judith C. Allan

Chapter 1

. . . whereas I was blind, now I see.

John 9:25

What is mental telepathy?
Is it intuition?
Is it a science?
Does it actually exist?
How does it manifest?
Must you practice some secret rite?
Is it a power for good?
For self-improvement?
For self-destruction?

Have you had some strange experience that you cannot explain?

How can you harness it?

How do you set about to make it work for you?

How have others done it—using it constantly in their lives until mental telepathy becomes an accepted sensory adjunct as natural as breathing, seeing, and smelling?

The following story is told of Mark Twain, who regarded his numerous manifestations much in the light of everyday occurrences.

One night, while he was lying in bed, an idea suddenly came to him. Why not a book with the silver mines of Nevada as its theme? The idea unfolded in every detail. He was even given the title for the book. He was instructed to call it *The Great Bonanza*.

Mark Twain awoke and drafted the manuscript. He had the urge to send it west to a fellow reporter who had once worked on the same paper with him. He composed a suitable letter.

He was about to mail it, when he decided that perhaps he had better contact the publisher first, in the event the book might not be accepted.

Another thought now struck him with overpowering intensity. In a flash of telepathy, he had the premonition that he would hear from his correspondent. So he pigeonholed both the book and the letter and wrote to the publisher.

Sure enough, his hunch was substantiated. A letter arrived from his friend in Nevada. Its contents corresponded with everything Mark Twain had written. The outline for the book corresponded with his own, complete even to the unusual title, *The Great Bonanza.*

Since these two men had not been in touch with each other for several years, what explanation except the power of an intense thought experienced simultaneously, could explain the sending and receiving of an idea through space and its crossing the continent on the same day at the same hour?

Mark Twain had many similar experiences involving mental telepathy. He had only to think of a person to make the contact in person. Once, while on a visit to Washington, he registered at the Arlington Hotel. He finished a leisurely dinner, read for a while, enjoyed a smoke, then decided to take a walk in the rain.

Whom could he visit to break his spell of loneliness?

All at once he remembered that an old friend of his lived in the city. Since it was already midnight, it was too late to call him or drop in for a visit, but the desire to see him, though brushed aside momentarily, sank deep into his subconscious mind.

An hour later he had the urge to replenish his stock of tobacco. He stepped into the neighboring cigar store, made a purchase, and exchanged some idle conversation with the proprietor. He was about to return to his room when suddenly he was seized by a strong impulse to go out into the street, in spite of the pouring rain. Ten steps would do it, his mind told him, urging him to obey.

He was walking along, seemingly without rhyme or reason, when his progress was impeded by two immense umbrellas coming toward him on the sidewalk. His profuse apology was rewarded by the sound of a familiar voice. The umbrella lifted and Mark Twain saw the face of the Washington friend he had thought of only moments before.

This encounter taking place in an unusual fashion at an odd hour of the night was another manifestation of mental telepathy.

Mental telepathy acts as an unpredictable force.

It may respond to intuition—as in the case of Mark Twain. It may behave as the obedient servant of the subconscious mind. It may form something out of nothing more than a thought or a desire on your part.

Did you ever try the experiment of sending your thought through space accompanied by your look?

You select a person whose back is turned to you. He may be walking on the street or seated in a lecture hall. However, as you concentrate your thought, the atomic energy flowing from your mind will strike your target, forcing your subject to be motivated into action and turn around to stare directly at you.

Baron Fersen, the great metaphysician, described his method of using mental telepathy to demonstrate the power in the eye.

He would pick a person in the crowd ahead. Then he would send out the command to turn, aiming it at a designated victim. Invariably, the person would then turn around and either smile or frown at Fersen, proving that he had received the mental stimulus within seconds of the signal.

My studies with Baron Fersen ultimately resulted in my being able to communicate with a human target just as he did. This took practice—as it may or may not in your case. Some people are more powerful than others.

The street is a good arena in which to test yourself. So is the crowded theatre, particularly when you find yourself annoyed by a lady of fashion whose gigantic hat or hairdo obscures your view of the stage. Speak to the lady—mentally, of course. Be sure to address her hat or hairdo. She will be certain to turn around in order to see who has tapped her on the shoulder, as it were, requesting that she remove the proverbial mountain that mars your vision.

Mental telepathy has numerous spokes in

its wheels. It can bring you either a rosebush or lilies.

I will never forget the irrevocable proof of the exact working of the mind.

An admirer of mine sent me a sheaf of Easter lilies. What I really longed to have in the way of flowers was a rosebush for my terrace. My desire was so intense that it must have reached the florist when he filled out the order. Someone else got the lilies intended for me and the rosebush arrived for my terrace, much to my friend's surprise.

Mental telepathy is often put to good use by actors, singers, politicians and lecturers.

Billy Sunday never thought of delivering one of his bombastic lectures prior to rehearsing it in advance in front of his mirror. He would roar, bellow, rant and shout, accompanying his words with dramatic gestures, in order to impress upon his subconscious mind every nuance, every word of his message. His subconscious mind was thus instructed to receive the message with exact recall when it came time to appear in front of his audience.

Caruso followed the same technique.

He would plant himself in front of his dressing-room mirror and sing to himself in a loud, commanding voice the single phrase, "I am Caruso! I am Caruso! I am Caruso!" In this way, he fixed the image of his greatness upon his subconscious mind, with the command to give a great performance.

There was no mistake about it. He was the great Caruso. He knew it. The audience knew it. And the world knew it.

The celebrated Dunninger was another example of mental telepathy set to work to produce results in an exacting career.

Dunninger became so adept at mental telepathy that he was able to reproduce the design of an engine created by Steinmetz even though the engine was carefully boxed and enveloped in numerous wrappings. In spite of all these precautions, Dunninger was able to report every detail of what lay inside. His intricate description of the contents amazed his audience.

Dunninger's story is a fascinating one. He developed his skill at mental telepathy as a boy in school.

Apparently, he was a very poor scholar. Arithmetic was his nemesis. He was always at the bottom of the class in this particular subject.

One day, the tide turned. His grades improved in some miraculous fashion. His teacher was mystified when he told her that he was not studying at home. He arrived at his answers by guesswork. He would reach for the right solutions in a mood of expectancy. The answers would come to him out of thin air in a way that he could not explain.

Actually, what Dunninger was doing in the classroom was something he would utilize later on in his life work in the theatre. Now, in the classroom, he collected the thoughts of his fellow students, tapping them for the right answers to the arithmetic problems.

Once he found himself able to work the technique, he tested it at the age of eighteen, using adults as his target.

Here, on the stage, he did the same mind-reading stunt. He would face the audience, gather up its thoughts telepathically, and issue the correct responses to the questions being volleyed at him. In this way he both intrigued and amazed his audiences.

Of course, you must have faith in your capacity to harness mental telepathy and make it serve you in your life. Both great and small achievements all have their birth in faith.

You cannot get up from a chair and cross the room unless you believe you can walk. You cannot open your mouth to speak without believing the words will come. You cannot dispute the fact that the dinner you eat will go through the proper stages of digestion, or you get indigestion.

Mental telepathy more or less follows the same subjective pattern. All human beings are

TRINITY.

endowed with intuition. A flash, a feeling known as inspiration comes at a time when you least expect it.

The familiar adage, "Speak of the devil and he's sure to appear" has a great deal of truth in it.

You think of a person. He appears on the scene like a puppet on a string, brought before your unbelieving eyes as if by some miracle in outer space.

You pick up the telephone to call a friend. Your friend is calling you at the very same moment.

You send a letter to someone at a distance. Your letters cross in the mail.

Your every thought, if properly trained, is a step in your journey toward acquiring the knack of turning on the very useful power contained in mental telepathy.

Mental telepathy can play a major role in your affairs. It can lead you to new avenues of endeavor.

How?

You have a conscious mind. You have a subconscious mind. You have a superconscious mind. These minds have access to the Greater Mind contained in the universe.

XX The conscious mind alone will not achieve your objective. XX

You must learn the proper use of the trinity

of your three minds. You must sharpen every faculty of your being.

Add the arrow of mental telepathy to your bow and you will have an important ingredient to help you in achieving health, harmony, happiness, and all the other riches you desire to manifest in your own life, as well as to help the lives of others in the world.

Chapter 2

*But let every man prove his own work,
and then shall he have rejoicing in himself
alone, and not in another.*

Galatians 6:4

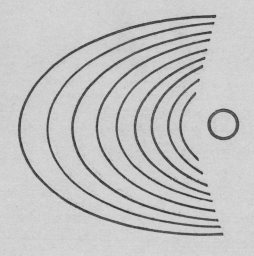

A hundred years ago a lot of dreaming fools said we would be talking across continents by means of invisible waves, diving in ships to the bottom of the ocean with men able to breathe in the depths below, riding in planes to the top of the sky at incredible speed, and maybe even going to the moon.

A hundred years ago the human race would have regarded radio, television, and X-rays as forms of witchcraft too wicked with which to meddle.

Marconi was incarcerated in a mental institution for two years because he insisted that sound existed in space. What's more, he intended to harness it and bring it into the home.

Not only inventors but philosophers have been unjustly crucified, ostracized by society, urged to recant their belief in the so-called unholy practice of the occult, and at the time of death were urged to retract their words. Many refused and chose to die branded as heathens and outcasts instead.

However, no truth is ever lost. No thought is ever erased from the blackboard of the universe. It continues to exist just as the sound and fury of the battles of old are still present in the atmosphere or ether. The ether banks everything. It contains everything ever created from the beginning of time.

It is in the ether that ideas float freely, awaiting appropriation at the hands of man.

An idea may intrigue an inventor. It may set a story on fire in the brain of a writer. It may ultimately braid the talents of both, producing visible proof that thoughts become things.

Jules Verne was famous for his amazing imagination. It was Verne, who, nearly a hundred years ago, wrote that masterpiece of the mind, *Twenty Thousand Leagues Under the Sea*. His pen described the world's first submarine. He wrote of dirigibles and helicopters long before they were in existence. His fertile mind conceived radio and television.

His ideas did not remain stillborn for long. Practical men put them to practical use. Today we have in our midst what was only the shadow of a thought emerging from a pen.

If thought power is good for anything it is good for everything.

If it can produce one thing for you it can produce all things. Nothing can stop you from thinking. You can think what you please. And, if to think is to form, then you can form what you please. This being so, you form your limitations in precisely the same way as you create your triumphs. Results, both positive and negative, are obtained when you think power into them.

When you say "I am," you send the vibrations of your thought currents into the ether to do your bidding as you see it done.

Mental telepathy plays a part in every situation. It is like Aladdin's lamp which you rub in order to make manifest a crust of bread or a kingdom. It will reproduce exactly what you conceive mentally.

The story is told of a comic who, prior to boarding a plane, applied for flight insurance, giving Heaven as his home address. The psychic powers proceeded to fulfill his request. The

d'où le grand danger de penser : I am a failure. !!! ou "Je ne réussirai jamais" !!!

plane crashed, and, as per his specifications, he reached the home he had designated.

There are no accidents in psychic power. It functions with mathematical precision. You create it, and it delivers just what you order in your mind.

An ultimate disaster that one man brought upon himself is an example of the negative application in self-involved mental telepathy. Allerton, the man in the case, began as a nonentity in a grocery chain. Then slowly, much to his personal gratification, he climbed the ladder of success. One day, an insurance broker approached him with a tempting "noncancelable health insurance policy." It provided so much a month as long as the insured was sick, no matter how long the duration.

He was a healthy man at the time. But the "noncancelable" policy intrigued him. Then his business began to fail. Fear crept into his heart. He had an impulse to read up on the heart and its ailments. This in itself was dangerous.

His mind began to fasten upon symptoms that were not even present in his body. He began to haunt the office of his doctor, with the idea of fraud uppermost in his thinking.

Eventually, in order to play the part most effectively, he took to his bed. The insurance company began to pay him the heavy sick benefits stipulated in his policy.

Allerton did not realize the effect of his dishonesty upon the subconscious mind, which is amenable to all suggestions.

His play-acting produced the reality of a man experiencing heart failure. No, he did not benefit from the money he was receiving at the hands of the insurance company. His death was self-imposed.

Thoughts are things. In fact, thoughts are objects. This has been proven by experiments conducted at Johns Hopkins University.

Scientists working in laboratories both here and abroad have weighed thoughts on a wonderful instrument known as an electro-encephalograph. They have established that thoughts contain body and are the result of mental action harnessed to electrical energy.

You originate thought. Since thoughts are creative, you can create for yourself the things you desire. Your only limit is that which you place upon it in your capacity to receive a greater portion of good.

The glass conductor that we see today on telephone poles which is responsible for carrying messages across vast distances had a humble beginning in an ordinary pocketknife.

The idea was given to Pupin, one of the greatest scientists in the world.

Pupin was born in Serbia of poverty-stricken parents. He spent his childhood herding sheep. The countryside was wild and lonely and infested with predatory animals. He and his brother lived in constant fear of being attacked by wolves.

One day, he devised a way to signal his brother at a distance. He had accidentally discovered that metal could be made to produce a sound wave. By plunging his pocketknife into the earth, he could send his brother a message. Thus the glass conductor that conveys messages over today's telephone, as well as other essential parts that go into making radios, was developed from a small boy's pocketknife.

Ideas respect neither person, place, nor thing. They can have their birth deep in the mind where silence prevails. They can travel by way of sound, both human and mechanical. They can even be transmitted from animal to man.

The cotton gin that revolutionized the industry of the South came about as the result of Eli Whitney watching his pet cat trying to reach through the bars of a cage to get at a canary. In a flash of insight, Whitney visualized steel prongs holding the cottonseed while iron claws drew the fluffy, white cotton out between the bars.

Imagination coupled with mental telepathy stimulated man to produce the printing press, the automobile, the typewriter, and countless other mechanical devices.

It created the two hundred inch telescope at

Mt. Palomar, as well as the spaceship that went to the moon.

Thought is a mode of motion, carried by the law of vibration and transmitted the same way as light and electricity.

Your mind is always capable of being directed by you—impressed by your authority to move in any direction you desire.

Turn your thought, no matter how wild or preposterous it may seem, out into the ether. Then wait for the answer. You can trust the Universal Mind to show you the way.

The Bible states:

For herein is the Father glorified—that ye bear much fruit.

Does this not imply that a world in which everything exists in such profusion would rejoice in your acceptance of its limitless harvest?

Chapter 3

Now faith is the substance of things hoped for, the evidence of things not seen.

Hebrews 11:1

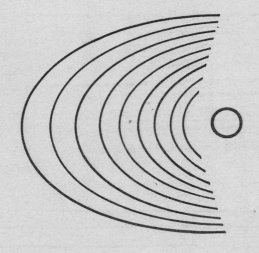

Various scientists have made diverse claims ascribing various faculties to the human mind. However, all concede that it is amazing in scope, unique in content, and the greatest work fashioned by the hand of the Infinite.

The celebrated Jung claimed not only that the subconscious mind contained all the knowledge it had gathered during the lifetime of the individual, but that it recorded all the wisdom of past ages.

He advanced a firm conviction that the subconscious mind was the connecting link between the human and the Universal Mind. According to Jung, the conscious mind had still another function.

He believed that by proper application of the conscious mind, man could appropriate the gifts of the universe itself.

He further contended that when the human mind was released from its outer environment, it was enabled to perceive far horizons as well as circumvent accepted laws.

Science has proven beyond a doubt that the subconscious mind is a vast magnet, with the power to draw upon the storehouse of the Universal Mind. It can produce unlimited knowledge concerning the people and events around you.

A sharpened intuition inevitably proves to be your willing servant. Learn to focus your thinking. It is an important tool. Careless thinking produces few or no results. Concrete thoughts bring about a high degree of certainty.

When you think intensely, you act upon the invisible which is made visible to you. This takes both practice and patience.

An intense thought can actually be seen.

It forms tiny magnetic lines which reach into the ether.

These lines resemble blue rays of light and connect you with the person or thing that is the instrument you are reaching for at the moment.

Sometimes this instrument is another ego which utilizes telepathy to send you an answer. Perhaps the power employs a material agency to connect you with the subject you desire to contact.

You may receive an invitation to attend a meeting.

You may hear an inner voice sent to you in warning.

You may hear an outer voice asking for your help. A situation that concerns you may call out to you.

In each instance, mental telepathy is at work.

There is a famous story about Emanuel Swedenborg, Swedish philosopher and theologian, that shows telepathy to be an established fact. Here is an example of thought transference in which distance proved no deterrent.

One evening, while dining with some friends in Gothenburg, some three hundred miles from his native city of Stockholm, Swedenborg suddenly announced that a fire had broken out there. A little later on he added that the fire had already burned the home of one of his neighbors and was threatening to consume his own home. His audience remained skeptical as he reported further developments. Later he insisted that the fire was finally brought under control only three doors from his own.

Subsequently, Swedenborg's report was confirmed by witnesses who stated that the fire had begun to blaze at the exact hour he received the impression and that it had been checked exactly three doors down the street from his house.

Of course, in Swedenborg's case, the ability to sense what happened at a distance came as a direct result of a faculty he had developed over the years. However, moments of crisis will also heighten your perception and raise the curtain to a sudden, distant vision or on a call for help from someone near and dear to you.

A crisis in the life of a human being or a nation seems to accelerate the long-distance message that travels through on its own wavelength without any apparent physical means.

Frequently incidents of mental telepathy take place on the scene of war.

This story is told about a young captain who was about to lead his men into battle.

There was no moon in the sky. He could not see more than a yard ahead of him. But as he took his first step forward, he heard his mother, thousands of miles away, cry out to him to take care. None of the others heard that voice. However, he ordered a halt, waiting for dawn. It was then that he saw the danger—the field that lay ahead was planted with mines.

Of course, his mother *had* called to him. Months later, after he reached home, she told him how she had been shaken out of sleep on that very night, at that very hour, by the vision of the danger that threatened him. She had risen from bed and spent the night in prayer for his safety.

Often, at the point of death, particularly on a battlefield, the picture of a loved one will make its sudden appearance to a close friend or relative in the land of the living.

The theory that mental telepathy is at work between sympathetic souls is frequently advanced by the facts in the case. There is no question that when one is at the point of death, memory takes over and reaches out to someone with whom there is a bond.

The dying soldier thinks of his mother. The machinery in the brain enlarges the picture and throws it into focus, creating a brain image of the loved one. This image passes through the waves of etheric space and even if the receiver is busy with other affairs, the sudden impact of the transferred thought reaches its mark and produces an effect. So the mother, who may believe she has witnessed a ghost or a spirit, is actually seeing a mental projection of her boy at the time of his death. This is proven by the fact that seeing is not in the eye. Seeing is in the brain. Her son's picture was impinged upon her brain.

It is in the brain that memories continue to exist. The ether of space vibrations is present everywhere. These vibrations were in the dead man's brain just as vividly as they were in the living brain of his mother. Distance is no deterrent. The picture remains in focus even at death. Brain cells do not disintegrate, nor does it matter whether the picture sent via mental telepathy comes from the living to the dead or from the dead to the living.

The reaching out in time of need is no doubt familiar to you. It is a frequent occurrence. Recently the press related the story of a young sailor who called out to his wife for help.

At the time, he was trapped in a submarine which lay helpless on the bottom of the sea. The machinery had refused to respond. Oxygen was almost at an end. The commanding officer informed the men that their situation was hopeless. Opiates were distributed so that death would be painless.

All at once, the young sailor fell over. The opiate had taken effect. As he dropped, he reached to embrace his wife. He saw her face clearly. At that moment, one of the broken controls of the submarine's machinery began to turn over. In falling, he had struck a certain bolt. The submarine surfaced. The "dead" were returned to life.

Thousands of similar cases have been reported by people who have seen a son, husband, or brother at the instant of danger, or a serviceman at the point of death.

These stories cannot be doubted since the sources are reputable.

The cases are always substantiated by comparing the evidence at hand.

How is such a vision projected?

How is it made manifest?

No doubt you have had the experience of suddenly hearing the voice of someone you know interrupt you at your work. It may involve an important issue or concern nothing more than the location of a lost hammer.

One incident concerns an important executive who virtually leaped to his feet in the midst of a directors' meeting. He had heard the imperious voice of his wife at home, who was in need of a hammer. He had been the last one to use it. "Where is it?" she demanded.

The executive switched on his human radio to inform her to look in the right-hand cupboard over the sink where he had inadvertently left it after using it the night before last.

She heard. She looked. She found the hammer.

Later on that evening, the wife and the

husband checked with each other to make sure
they had not been dreaming.

How was this feat accomplished?

There is no doubt that when you concentrate
on a matter that is important to you, your
intuitive powers will be set in operation. The
answer will come in the nature of information,
or an urge to do or say something that will
prove successful.

Married couples have often reported their
successful application of mental telepathy.

A husband about to board a train for home
and suppertime receives a message to please
be sure to stop at the grocer's and buy a loaf
of bread. He obeys the impulse. He is met
upon arrival by his wife, who acknowledges
that she was short of bread. Yes, she had sent
him the message, certain he would pick up the
mental telephone and make the purchase.

How is this done?

It is essential that you cultivate and develop
your intuition. To do so, recognize and
appreciate any inner urge which taps your consciousness like a soft hand on your shoulder.
If the intuitive visitor is given a welcome, he
will come again. The more cordially you receive him, the more frequent his visits. Ignore
or neglect your intuition, and it will leave you.

This is to be deplored since your intuitive
faculty protects you, inspires you, and serves
you in innumerable ways, manifesting itself in

sparks of mental telepathy nothing short of miraculous.

You are guided into making important decisions.

You are led up one road in preference to another.

Warnings which may affect your friends and your family are often telegraphed seemingly from out of the blue.

One day in church, our organist stopped playing a hymn to run to the pulpit and announce that the excursion boat carrying our youngsters on a Sunday-school picnic was in danger of sinking in the storm that was rising in the bay. She pleaded with the minister to stop the service, and she asked the congregation to kneel in prayer.

Her request was considered erratic by many in the congregation. However, she insisted that only interceding prayer would save the youngsters.

Her intuition proved the working powers of mental telepathy. Prayer effected the rescue of the boat that was sinking in the bay. After all, was it not prayer invoked by Rickenbacker and his men floating helpless and starving on a raft that caused a bird to land on Rickenbacker's head, providing the men with food?

No doubt, warnings have reached you by a telegraph signal you cannot explain.

Perhaps you are driving along, thinking of

nothing in particular, your eyes on the road ahead. Say you are moving at a high speed. You get the sudden urge to slow down as you come to the curve below. Then you see why you were given the warning. You would have plowed into the wreck of a number of cars that had telescoped into each other at the bend.

Perhaps, without any apparent reason for doing so, since the street ahead is clear of traffic, you hear the inner command to put on your brake. Seconds later, a heavy truck comes rolling into view.

You would have been fatally struck if you had not stopped at that instant. Yet you were certain you had looked in all directions. The truck appeared as if from nowhere. But your psychic eye saw it for you and warned you in advance.

Here is mental telepathy at its best, the guardian angel who guides and cares for you, provided you acknowledge its invisible presence and praise it for every good deed that it performs for you.

Chapter 4

The righteousness of thy testimonies is everlasting: give me understanding, and I shall live.

Psalms 119:144

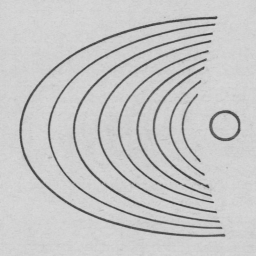

You live in a sea of universal energy in which your being is steeped.

This energy is everywhere. It envelops every human, every animal, every growing thing that lives and breathes, permeating every living being.

It is yours to tap and use. It is rich in content, inexhaustible, present in all places and in all time.

Just think of it! Think of a bank with unlimited resources at your command, its doors
wide open to you. And you are as necessary
to this power as this power is necessary to you.
Both must function for each other or both
would negate a law that operates in the
universe.

Ideas float freely about in the ether. These
are available to all. That is why human beings
tune in on similar ideas and produce similar
inventions, often simultaneously.

The printing press is a good illustration of
what takes place in outer space and is brought
to earth on a single beam. It was conceived by
two minds continents apart. Previously it lay
dormant. Then suddenly it was simultaneously
presented to the world during the same era.

The world functioned without a telegraph
for thousands of years. Then Henry in America, Wheatstone in England, Morse while at
sea, and a German scientist in Munich all came
forward with the invention a short time apart
from each other.

There is no doubt, for the records prove it,
that the idea for the telegraph was discovered
by men who not only did not know each other
personally but were not aware of each other's
work. Apparently this was an accident. But
there was the electric telegraph—there in the
ether—waiting to be born no matter who
reached out to perform the magic feat.

In the same way, etheric energy can be tapped by you and your individual mind.

You become what you imagine. You must see the outer world as a projection of your inner world. It is essential that you imagine yourself into the state of seeing your desire fulfilled. Your imagination will go about the business of producing the perfect likeness.

The old saying "As within so without" contains more than a mere semblance of truth.

You need not concern yourself with the ways and means. The devices best needed to realize your wish will make their appearance in due course, often in an amazing fashion.

Train your imagination to picture your life as you would like to see it made manifest. By the proper use of your imagination, you can acquire power to be anything and to have everything you want. Here is a powerful means of bringing you face-to-face with a tangible, workable method.

Imagination is the beginning of the pattern, the sowing of seeds that will result in future action.

Imagination was the tool in the unskilled hands of prehistoric man who covered the walls of his shelter with crude drawings of the food he needed in order to sustain life. No doubt he looked to his art to produce reality. His eye was focused on his walls morning, noon, and night. Here was the beginning of the modern highway billboard with its power of suggestion inveighing the senses of the passing motorist.

The Egyptians were adept in the art of picture-making. They built tombs for royalty, decorating them profusely with scenes depicting a life of honor, spoils, slaves, and success. All were eventually manifested.

The ancient Greeks practiced the preachment of beauty to women about to give birth. Art, statuary, flowers, perfume, all were provided in order to impress the subconscious mind of pregnancy with its promise that a lap of luxury awaited the arriving infant.

For centuries, prayer wheels, along with ardent praying, was the method used by Tibetan Buddhists to ask for benefits.

Great men have used the picture-making form of mental telepathy with amazing success in order to achieve the desired goal.

Napoleon saw himself as a soldier before he rode out to the battlefield. He imagined himself a commander at the head of the French army while he was still an infantryman.

Conrad Hilton fancied himself operating a hotel long before he ever owned one. As a boy, he pretended he was a successful hotel magnate and set up shop from a blueprint of dreams.

Gene Tunney prepared himself before he took on Jack Dempsey in the ring. Each day, right in his own home, many miles away from the arena, he fought an imaginary Dempsey. What's more, he studied the films made of Dempsey, rehearsing every move and practicing the countermove as if Dempsey were actually present.

He worked hard, urging his imagination toward perfection and an ultimate victory in the ring.

Imagination does not require any aid from the physical body. It can function on its own steam, using the mind as its tool.

There are concert pianists who seldom touch the keyboard. They practice mentally instead, imagining themselves performing before an audience. A champion such as Ben Hogan rehearsed his shots until perfect—all in his mind.

The story is told of the famous pole vaulter who was reprimanded by his coach for lounging in a hammock prior to participating in the Olympics. It was only after he had won the championship that he confessed he had not been resting in that hammock. He had been hard at work:—mentally pole-vaulting while apparently idling in the shade of that old apple tree!

A swimming teacher famous for producing swimming champions was interviewed one day by the press. Where was it he had learned his wonderful technique, the reporters asked. He confessed that he used his mother's kitchen for a pool. He merely sat back on an old kitchen chair. It was there he did his swimming!

Billy Graham acquired a dynamic personality through years of practice—in his mind—as he preached sermons to the cypress stumps in Florida. They were his only audience in the beginning.

Today, the huge assemblages of human beings he attracts can scarcely be computed.

Beginners are taught karate by practicing the art in slow, sustained motion, rehearsing each of the thrusts that will follow later in the actual exercise. This is to impress the subconscious with the method that is used to attain perfection.

No doubt, you know that your sense organs function as receivers. Your motor organs function as transmitters. Your mind controls both of these. That is why the proper use of your imagination is so potent a factor in your life.

Set that imagination of yours to work.

Imagine!

Visualize!

Assume the fulfilled dream!

When a farmer plants a field he cultivates it. The rains fall on it. The sun shines on it. It grows and grows until one day it is ready for the harvest.

Ask yourself just what you want out of life. Whenever you assume the picture of being what you want to be you are making an investment.

See yourself in the position of your dream fulfilled. Pretend that you are a new being, your every need already answered and in action.

What kind of house would you like to live in?

What kind of car would you like to drive?

What kind of clothes would you like to wear?

What kind of country club would you like to join?

What kind of friends would you like to have?

How much wealth would you like to demonstrate?

Is it health?

Is it wisdom?

Set aside a period of several minutes each day where you can be alone and undisturbed. Relax. Make yourself comfortable.

Now close your eyes and exercise your imagination.

Now see within your mind a mental picture of your desire in its finished state. Send it out into space.

Give thanks that it is working for you and is certain to hit its target.

Chapter **5**

Thou shalt also decree a thing, and it shall be established unto thee: and the light shall shine upon thy ways.

Job 22:28

What is mental telepathy?

This was the question which the amazing Harold Sherman asked himself prior to the extraordinary pioneering experiments he conducted with Sir Hubert Wilkins, the explorer.

Was there a mental ether, containing thought waves and resembling radio waves, traveling through space?

Could people prove their capacity to be

sending and receiving sets? Could images be
transmitted between them?

In his remarkable book *Thoughts Through
Space* Mr. Sherman recorded the ESP sessions
between himself and Sir Hubert with thousands of miles between them. These findings
were later checked for accuracy. The high
percentage of Mr. Sherman's "hits" surprised
the whole world.

He came to the conclusion that long-distance
telepathy between two people was possible.
The images most strongly felt by Wilkins were
those most accurately recorded by Sherman.
In other words, intensity plays an important
role in mental telepathy, seemingly sending the
thought waves or impulses at a faster pace and
in a more accurate manner.

While this may be the method best employed
for Mr. Sherman, your faculties may not respond in precisely the same way. You may not
need to sit down for a nightly session of concentration.

A certain Westchester housewife, often con-
sulted by the police to help them solve their
murder cases, does not turn on her powers for
long hours on end. She does not go into
meditation. She controls a sort of mental radio
by merely pushing a button until she finds the
right station. Then she concentrates in a relaxed manner, trying to find out what has
taken place and where.

She works at her mental radio in the midst of her housework—while doing dishes, feeding the children, or vacuuming her living room. Meanwhile, she sends out the thought that produces the picture that she needs to present to the police.

In one case, she received a very vivid impression of both the criminal and the crime.

The man in the case had murdered the woman of the house, hiding the gun he had used under a log close by.

In a vivid succession of pictures given to her like frames in a film, she saw first the house, then the lawn that had been disturbed in order to bury the weapon under the log. The police checked her findings. They located the log, found the gun, and eventually caught up with the criminal.

The famous psychic Florence who recently passed away, operated in New Jersey and worked very closely with the authorities, furnishing clues on cases which the law conceded had proven too baffling for the ordinary mind. She worked mainly by visualization—picture-making—bringing about vivid impressions.

At times, she required some personal belonging such as a shoe, purse, scarf, or sock which she insisted furnished her with the vibrations she needed for her work. (The article might belong to the victim or be the clue left behind by the marauder.) In either case,

Florence claimed that the vibrations were still
there in the form of emanations that could be
used as guide posts by her subconscious mind
to arrive at her conclusions. These were very
often startling, and the police held Florence in
the highest regard.

There is no doubt that you can learn to
operate your own mental radio in a fashion
best suited for your purpose.

Claude Bristol, author of *The Magic of
Believing,* gave his method of using mental
telepathy in order to obtain a needed ladder,
a quota sale of pies, or something as mundane
as a parking space for his car.

He saw that space in his mind's eye long before he made his demand. Although he might
approach a long line of cars with no opening
available, someone was sure to ride off in the
nick of time—as if on signal—to make room
for him and his vehicle.

In his *Edinburgh Lectures on Mental Science,* Judge Thomas Troward presents the
theory that if you create a spiritual prototype
by the mere operation of your thought—believing that your desire has already been fulfilled—the accomplishment will follow as a
matter of course. You create a nucleus which,
like a magnet, attracts the iron filings necessary
for fulfillment.

Needless to say, imagination is a prime requisite.

How can you change some condition in your life that you do not want?

By *imagination*.

How can you create some condition you would you like to see take place in your life?

By *imagination*.

One way of doing this is to imagine yourself behind a camera. You are going to take a picture. The object you want—condition, money, trip, house, wife that you want, as well as the success that you want to manifest—is the picture you intend to photograph. This represents your negative. The negative is the power contained in your subconscious mind.

You hold your camera in place. You focus the lens on the picture you have in your mind. You press the button and impress the picture as vividly as possible upon your subconscious mind. Your work is done.

You have captured the image you desire. It has not only left its mark upon that subconscious mind of yours—with the command to produce a perfect likeness—but your camera has also simultaneously impressed the subjective mind of the universe, which is where the actual work of manifestation will take place. It received your negative and will ultimately deliver the positive picture.

The finished picture will subsequently be produced and made visible to you in your world.

Chapter 6

. . . *for there is nothing covered, that shall not be revealed; and hid, that shall not be known.*

Matthew 10:26

William James, the famous Harvard psychologist, estimated that the average man uses only ten percent of his mental powers.

The rest is at a standstill—a matter of sheer waste—poverty in the presence of the greatest wealth in the universe.

Mankind bemoans the loss of its forests. It worries us that the supply of oil and coal may dwindle and come to an end. But the greatest waste of all lies in man himself: in his misuse of the wealth in his mind.

You live in a sea of energy. The waters must ebb and flow in order for you to survive.

A sea that is static means death to all forms of life, including that of the human being.

An example of this is Palestine, which lays claim to two seas.

The Sea of Galilee is fed by the River Jordan, which has its source in the hills and flows south, emptying its waters into other bodies of water as it gives of itself. The Sea of Galilee contains fresh water. It is full of fish. It is beautiful to behold. Lush vegetation grows along its banks as it flows on and on.

However, the River Jordan spills into still another sea—the Dead Sea. This sea keeps every drop of water intact within its banks. Neither beast nor bird will drink of it. No green grows on its shores.

It receives without giving and because of this, like so many human beings, it is dead instead of alive.

It is dead because it has failed to realize that life is dynamic, not static. Life is always moving forward. It is not meant to stand still.

The universe considers stagnation in the nature of a sin and soon disposes of those who do not contribute to the world of being or have outgrown their usefulness.

The Brontosaurus which measured over

one hundred feet in length—the Tyrannosaurus which boasted the strength of a locomotive— the Pterodactyl—all those monsters of prehistoric ages disappeared not only because they outlived their functions but also because they could not meet the changing times adequately.

It was the same with the great cities of the past.

Empires like Rome and Greece fell before the onslaught of time.

China stood still for over a thousand years. Mistakenly she regarded herself as being snug and secure within the great walls behind which she had fortressed herself. She found only that she had been regressing instead of progressing.

What is the alternative?

How do you emerge from your shell?

How can you manifest whatever you desire?

You need not be poor.

You need not be a clod. You are not meant to spend your days at hard labor in return for food and shelter. You have unlimited potential. Within your being is a power which can lift you out of the rut. You must learn to use this power—this Mind that can achieve all things for you.

The story is told of a Maryland school teacher who put her slender knowledge of mental telepathy to work.

Miss Abby Jones was thirty-seven years old —when it happened.

Although she had taught geography for nearly twenty years, she had never in her life traveled any further than Pittsburgh, Pennsylvania. Her name would never make history either, for like millions of others in the world she lived an assembly-line existence.

She got up in the morning, dressed, breakfasted, and went to work. She came home from work, ate her supper, and went to bed in order to get up to work again.

One day, as if by accident, a chance conversation changed her whole life. The teachers were all together having lunch for the last time. Today was graduation. Tomorrow was vacation.

"Where are you going for the summer?" one of them asked Miss Jones. "Who knows? Maybe you'll meet a millionaire!"

Her answer shot out like a bullet: "You're right! Why shouldn't I meet and marry a millionaire?"

Everyone laughed. No wonder. Miss Jones had no figure. Miss Jones had no glamor. Her clothes were drab. Her chest was flat. She wore old-fashioned, horn-rimmed spectacles.

But a dream now stirred in her heart. From now on, she was through seeing America from a big blue map. She was going to cross its great rivers, climb its highest mountains, and tour its tall cities in person. What's more, she was going to wear a gold ring on her finger and change her hated status of old maid to that of being a happily married wife.

But mental telepathy requires more than a dream. You must do something about it.

If you want water, you must dig a ditch. If you pray for rain, be sure to carry an umbrella. If you want a husband, it's not enough to wish for him. You must do something about it.

Miss Jones took action.

She bought new clothes and learned how to wear them. She groomed her figure. She haunted the local beauty parlor. She had been making a living. Now she was making a life.

Each year in the past, Abby had spent her vacation in exactly the same way. She visited her sister who had a farm just outside of Scranton, Pennsylvania. There were no virile males around. There were no millionaires growing like apples on the trees in the old family orchard.

Finally Miss Jones looked her new part. Now she had to play it. How could a fish be coaxed to the hook?

Times had changed since Mother was a girl. You couldn't catch a man by sitting home in the parlor, pouring tea, painting china, and waiting for a beau. According to the census bureau, there were now nearly two unmarried women for every unattached male in America.

The times were not propitious for an old maid whose dream was marriage. She cast about for an inspiration. How about going on a trip? How about California?

And so Miss Jones went to California only to discover that although it was the land of fragrant orange blossoms, she would never wear them on her wedding veil. In sunny California, most of the men were safely married and the few eligibles could only be had at a premium she was not prepared to pay.

So Miss Jones returned East. She still had two weeks left of her vacation and she decided she might as well visit her sister. She bought a ticket and boarded a train for Scranton. It was a warm summer night and she drowsed off. She was awakened by a tap on the shoulder.

It was the conductor. He told her that she had passed her station. There was nothing she could do but get off, cross the tracks, and wait for a train back.

By now it was midnight. There is nothing more dreary or terrifying than a dark, deserted country railroad station. The shadows were deep, the mosquitos thick. There was no bench, so she sat down on her suitcase. She was all alone in what seemed a very lonely world.

Suddenly the wind went out of her sails. Discouragement seized her. Everybody gets discouraged. Often, just before a big achievement, you are faced with apparent failure. She thought of her dream, her silly dream of meeting and marrying a millionaire.

Her mind began to argue with her heart. Her mind said, "Abby, you've been a fool. You'll never get married. It's an impossibility!"

Her heart said, "Nothing is impossible provided you believe."

Her mind retorted, "Wait till you get back to school. You'll get a horselaugh all right when they see your gamin haircut. And you'd better get rid of your costume jewelry and give away your open-work sandals. Incidentally, your old glasses are still in the top drawer of your desk."

An express train roared by and enveloped her in smoke, thick, gray, like fog. Her life again was a fog. Two hot tears rolled down her cheeks. All at once, she was tired of everything, tired of living, tired of working, and even tired of dreaming such a foolish dream as being married—a destiny that is every woman's birthright.

Then rebellion set in. Why not achieve her dream? Her intuition had brought her this far. She would trust it to guide her to her goal. Somewhere, somehow, she decided, her dream would materialize.

" JE RÉUSSIRAI envers et contre tout. !

Again went the message, moving toward its destination by the invisible wires of her thought waves.

It was two or three o'clock in the morning, and she was weary. She drowsed off again.

This time she was awakened by the sound of a human whistle. She looked up. There was the most handsome man she had ever seen looking down on her in amazement.

"What are you doing here?" he was saying to her.

"What are *you* doing here?" she retorted.

And he said, "I wish I knew. I'm stopping at the house of some friends of mine about three miles away in the hills. We were having a cocktail party when I began getting bored for no reason whatsoever.

"Then I got the sudden message to get out and start walking. I seemed to be propelled by an unseen hand that took me down one street and up another till I came here to the station. Don't ask me why. And here I am— and here you are," he added, "as if by accident."

But she knew better. It was no accident. There are no accidents in life. It was no accident that he was a widower with vast chainstore interests which took him all over the country and that he found traveling alone lonely.

Each man is the architect of his own life.

Miss Jones made a blueprint of a dream, and the bricks came out of the blue to complete the dream.

By the law of attraction which respects a sincere desire, two people will be brought together, from opposite sides of the world if necessary, because if you believe something strongly enough and do something about it, no one and nothing can stop your dream from coming true for you, provided you tune in on mental telepathy and trust it to do the job!

"NOTRE MARRIAGE."

Chapter 7

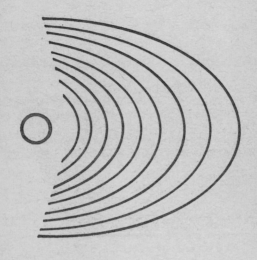

And Stephen, full of faith and power, did great wonders and miracles among the people.

Acts 6:8

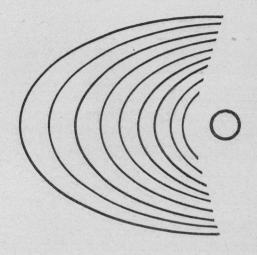

It was Kant, the celebrated German philosopher, who claimed that two achievements were outstanding in God's remarkable universe.

The first of these was the heaven above the earth, studded with its scintillating, mysterious stars. The second of these was the mind of man and what lay within the human brain.

Man's knowledge of his physical world has accelerated at a breathless pace throughout the centuries. He has learned to build impressive bridges which span the widest of rivers, yet he has failed to span the narrow channel which might lead him to find out who he is, why he lives, why he suffers, and why he dies.

He has built railroads across many miles of continent, yet he cannot cross the continent which still lies unexplored in the greater expanse of his mind.

The astronomer can bring the star in farthest space within vision of his telescope, yet he cannot turn the telescope upon his own life and reach a scientific conclusion.

The geologist chooses to concentrate all his efforts upon what makes the earth, and in his search he arrives at the answer he seeks. Yet does he pause long enough in his work to ask himself what makes the geologist?

You know how your car operates. You have tinkered with the engine and at times succeeded in repairing it.

How about your inner self? Do you know how it works? Can you repair that, too?

Do you realize—with a sense of pride— that your own mind is an engine of untold power, and your thought is the ruler and creator of all forms of life, of all events in your universe? Physical energy cannot compare with the omnipotence of thought because it is the latter that enables man to harness all else, making it operate to produce results.

Il faut SAVOIR ce que l'on VEUT !

It is acknowledged that men are dynamos. But even the dynamo can do nothing by itself. The mind must work the dynamo. It is only then is it useful and its energy finds a channel.

What has all of this to do with mental telepathy?

Most people float like straws on the river of life, drifting here and there and changing direction with every passing wind and wave.

That is why it is necessary to create a point of singleness from which you do not waver.

Daydreaming dissipates your energy. It destroys your psychic forces. That was why St. Dominic, the wise Castilian Friar, invented the rosary back in the twelfth century.

The telling of the beads had a definite object. No matter if the attention wandered during the repetition of the ten Hail Mary's, the eleventh bead, separate from the others and bigger than the rest, brought the mind back to its center.

Inner movement is the force by which outward events are brought to pass.

Effect is the result of cause. In order to produce any cause, you must guide your mind into the world of cause, a world that does not exist on the surface of thought but in the great powerhouse within you. Your mind must act beneath, above, and beyond the outer in order to produce the cause you desire to manifest.

A technique you can make your own is to choose a focal point. It can be a picture on a wall, the pleasant memory of some enchanting place, or something as strange as the ashes in a fireplace.

Leonardo da Vinci chose this means to concentrate even though the flame was gone. He would often sit and stare for hours at a heap of ashes. This would bring on a reverie in which would be born the inspiration he needed to proceed with his work.

Of course, confidence and faith will energize and stimulate the faculty of producing things out of thoughts. What's more, in order for a suggestion to be effective, it must be preceded by a mental vision of the object you wish to obtain. It must take direction from a strong desire. Your will must come into play. The word must be spoken. The action will follow.

And why is suggestion so powerful? Its potency is due to the fact that it gives a pattern to the conscious, which in turn is relayed to the subconscious, which in turn is relayed to the Universal Consciousness.

It is here that creation takes place. You must accept the fact that here—in the invisible—the visible is born.

There are various methods of using your intuitive powers to bring them into play.

The great Bernard Baruch harnessed his conscious mind to that of his subconscious. He utilized this form of teamwork when a seemingly unsolvable problem faced the nation,

sending out a message via mental telepathy to
attract the right people to his office. They came
in droves. He never rejected any advice that
arrived on the wings of the outer world, wel-
coming the opinions not only of his staff
members but of the steady stream of strangers
who called on him.

Here was the problem, he would confess in
all candor. Any suggestions?

Then he would listen, absorbing every word
that swirled about him, storing it away in his
subconscious mind. Repeatedly, he assured *his*
~~that~~ subconscious mind ~~of his~~ that he trusted
it completely.

The solution might come as a hunch.

But sometimes he carefully laid out all
the facts as if he were priming the pump.
Then all of a sudden, the machinery inside of
his head would start to accelerate. It would
move faster and faster until it began working
at top speed. All at once, the answer emerged
finished, perfect, complete.

This mental process was regarded as nothing
less than a miracle by the working psychologists whom he numbered among his friends.
They had the highest regard for Baruch's subconscious mind, acknowledging his position
as the nation's greatest financial advisor.

At times, Baruch would dream the answer
—as in the case of Mussel Shoals or the prob-

lem of Chilean nitrates which harassed the country.

According to Baruch, concentration did not mean merely thinking a thought but the transmutation of that thought into a practical form. He was correct in his theory.

When an idea takes form in consciousness and goes out from mind, it seeks to externalize itself. In this way, your dreams of today become the realities of tomorrow.

But what you visualize in mind must be vitalized. Your creative power must be activated to the point of magnetizing conditions around you and attracting the circumstances and resources necessary to the realization of your desires.

However, you must believe whatever you picture for yourself. You must put forth an earnest effort toward its achievement if you hope for an answer to your need.

Belief works. Without it no attainment is possible. The most powerful forces in the universe are invisible, beyond mortal sight, touch, or sound. Things reflect through matter, which is conceded to be a mass of vibrating atoms held together in the ether.

One night, Marconi was entertaining a friend in his laboratory. The two were discussing the intricate phases of wireless communication. At dawn, as they were leaving for home, the greatest inventor of his day turned to his guest and said:

"All my life I have been studying this phenomenon. But there is one thing I simply cannot understand about radio."

"Something you don't understand about radio?" echoed his friend unbelievingly.

"Yes," answered Marconi, "Radio. What is it?"

Chapter **8**

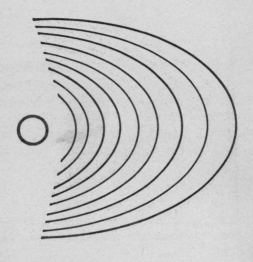

Thou wilt show me the path of life: in thy presence is fulness of joy; at thy right hand there are pleasures for evermore.

Psalms 16:11

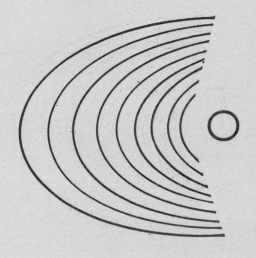

Dr. Elmer Gates, one of the greatest names in psychology, computed the ratio in the mind. He advanced the theory that it consisted of ninety-eight percent subconscious and only two percent conscious, a figure which amazed all mankind.

Freud, the Austrian physician and founder of psychoanalysis, labeled the libido as being a sign of the sex urge inherent in man.

Jung, who worked with Freud, insisted that man's mind went beyond the mere urge for sex, reaching out its ego in order to find some form of expression.

Adler, the final illustrious name in the trinity of great analysts, posed an even more involved theory in which the libido represented the inferiority complex in man, warring within him and forever questioning him as to whether he were capable of achieving and expressing.

Does it matter which of these viewpoints you choose to take? The important thing for you to remember is that your libido is simply your deep inner desire which is always eager to externalize itself and anxious to produce results for you.

However, you must face up to the fact that you are what you are because of your consciousness. The character of your thoughts has made you either a success or a failure.

Think in terms of mediocrity and you create a negative pattern. Success is born out of confidence. You cannot fail to objectify in the outer world what you have fashioned within. Your thoughts are the harvest you gather—not those you think now and then, but those that dominate your everyday life fastening themselves like barnacles on a boat which impedes its travels rather than speeds it on.

The well-known expression "As a man think-eth in his heart so is he" holds the clue to the solution of many of your difficulties. It is the way you think that produces the deed.

Mental telepathy can be used by the individual upon himself as well as sent into space. You are always the result of the im-pressions you have telegraphed to your sub-conscious mind.

It is an accepted fact that you are a psychic magnet, drawing constantly upon all that is in the universe.

Think wealth. You attract it.

Think success. You attract it.

Think health. You attract it.

Two men may be lying side by side in a hospital ward. Both have the same illness. Both are wheeled out to the operating room on the same day. Why then does one die while the other survives? Why is it that one returns and the other never comes back to the shore of the living?

What is the answer?

The medical men of today no longer close their minds to the powerful part that thought plays in curing the human body.

However, in the case of Mary Anderson, everyone had given up. It was only a matter of days before this patient would die. She lay in traction because her body had stopped pro-ducing the calcium needed in her system.

Her bones had become like glass. The least movement caused a break. Often when she was lifted in and out of bed, one of her ribs would crack.

Soon, she thought, it would be Christmas. Christmas—happiness, people, presents for everybody, even the dog.

But what could her husband buy her for Christmas, he asked, as he leaned over her bed. She could not wear a coat. She could not use a dress. She could not eat candy. And no patient in her condition could jingle jewelry.

Her eyes posed the same question.

What could she buy him for Christmas? What did he want most of all in the way of a Christmas gift?

Andy hesitated to answer.

Suddenly an impulse seized him. There at the window stood the bureau—the regulation white bureau of the sickroom. Upon that bureau was a soap dish, and in the soap dish was a cake of soap. A mirror hung over the bureau.

He crossed the room. He could not speak in words. But perhaps there was a way that he could tell his wife just what it was he wanted for a Christmas present from her.

He picked up the cake of soap and printed in very large letters upon the face of the glass:

HOME
FOR
CHRISTMAS

The nurse came in. She frowned when she saw what he had written. She hurried out to call in the doctor.

The doctor smiled indulgently and went away.

The words remained just as Andy had written them:

HOME
FOR
CHRISTMAS

All through that first night and the many nights that followed, when Mary could see nothing else, when life hung by a thread, those three words were electric in action—beseeching, arresting, commanding, compelling, pleading, speaking, dynamic, hypnotic—a love letter from the one man in her life.

Then it happened. Her subconscious was impressed to take action.

The night before Christmas, the telephone rang to summon Andy to the hospital. A Christmas gift was waiting for him. He must come at once to get it.

Of course, Mary's recovery was regarded

as a miracle. Nobody knew quite how it happened. She could go home for Christmas!

The hospital wheels went round; they needed the bed for an incoming patient.

The sequel to the story is even more heart-warming. Andy tried to buy the bureau. But for obvious reasons, the hospital would not sell it.

Then the truth was revealed.

Someone else had bought it—a Mr. Slocum for a Mrs. Slocum. He had changed the words to:

HOME
FOR
EASTER

and moved the bureau down the corridor into the room of his invalid wife.

The magic medicine is always present in the subconscious mind provided you impress upon it as Mary Anderson did. Night after night, hour upon hour, she sent the full charge of her vital forces toward the target of those three words which responded in accordance with psychic law.

And how was the healing accomplished?

No doubt, the subconscious mind took over, ready to respond to the call for help. After all, it is your subconscious mind that is in charge of all the intricate processes of digestion, assimilation, elimination, and circulation. Its knowledge of the secret workings of your body is beyond the wisdom of the wisest men of medicine.

Your subconscious mind built your body from the time you were a fetus in the womb. It assumed the intricate duties of your body's operation and repair. You were its main concern. Its numerous tasks were inculcated right from the start. It had a single objective—to keep you in perfect health.

Right from the start, while you were in the process of growing up—busy learning reading, writing, and arithmetic—your subconscious mind was already meeting problems that presented themselves in your body and were so gigantic in scope that no professor could have solved them.

These increased as you became an adult. Indisposition, illness, accident, broken limbs and damaged organs—all came to the clinic of that patient, wise, all-knowing, hard-working subconscious mind of yours. And with faith as the antidote these problems were solved.

How?

The story is told of a girl who fell from a swing when she was six years old. She injured her right leg so severely that it was inches shorter than her left leg.

However, she determined to correct her condition and brought her imagination into play, seeing herself perfect and whole.

This was the pattern she impressed upon her subconscious mind, feeding it constant encouragement.

Sure enough, the right leg began to grow, gradually at first. But by the time she reached the age of eighteen, she was able to discard the special shoe she had been forced to wear all through childhood.

Another striking incident is that of a hunchback whose spine had been injured at birth.

He, too, refused to accept his deformity. He decided he would be perfect in limb like the rest of his schoolmates. He charged his imagination with the image of growing into a tall, straight man, and he urged his subconscious mind to point out the ways and means to obtain his objective.

He was led to obey his intuition which suggested that he consult a physical culture instructor who would put him through a series of exercises.

His teacher had great patience as well as even greater vision. He saw his student straight and tall—just as the boy saw himself. He helped the boy practice hanging from the trapeze in order to straighten that crippled spinal column. The boy stretched and strengthened all the muscles of his back.

Little by little, he saw a new reflection in the

mirror. By the time he was grown he had eliminated his hump. He became a man six feet tall, with no sign of his earlier deformity.

Here was mental telepathy at its best, put to use through the power of the subconscious mind that is always a willing partner to any physical improvement.

The subconscious mind knows its inherent potentials. It knows that good is expected of it.

It is an obedient servant. And, so, it will also produce any problem you envision for it.

Are you a diet faddist?

Can you tell just how high your carbohydrate and protein intake should be at each meal? Do you count calories and vitamins?

Are you a stickler for scientific combinations?

Like everything else, your mode of eating is a mental process. The mind as well as the body requires the proper food.

Perhaps you are one of those perfectionists who watches your diet the way a cat watches a mouse. Yet when you sit down to your meals your mind sits down beside you, an unwelcome guest who seasons your fare with thoughts of worry, anxiety, doubt, and fear: Perhaps you are eating something you should not be eating. Perhaps that something will sour in your stomach and not agree with you. Perhaps you are eating too many carbohydrates

or too little protein, or too few calories or the
wrong kind of vitamins.

All the vitamins in the world will not benefit
you if you have harnessed the power of your
imagination to negatives. The subconscious
mind will deliver your order exactly as you
dictate.

Of course, well-balanced meals benefit the
body. But a scientific consciousness is far more
important than the diet you favor.

The power of the mind to make use of
mental telepathy produces not only health in
place of sickness, but wealth in place of
poverty.

The story is told of a businessman who
opened a "hole in the wall" to sell typewriters.

He did not advertise.

He did not solicit.

Yet his business flourished like the proverbial bay tree, as a result of the mental
telepathy he applied each and every morning
when he put his key into the door of his tiny
domain. He would stand at the threshold for a
few moments of silent prayer, envisioning his
place full of customers who had come to buy
typewriters. In his mind, he heard the telephone ringing. Customers were clamoring for
adding machines. One day, he told himself, he
would add these to his stock.

Of course, that day came.

As a result of his disciplined practice of

seeing himself busy and prosperous, his business expanded until that "hole in the wall" became a whole floor and finally a skyscraper on Park Avenue.

Mankind suffers from various problems which may be health, lack of supply, friendship, companionship, love, or the right life work.

Perhaps you are troubled because you have no definite goal in life, or the wrong sort of goal. You have no aim except to spend money, compete with your neighbor, join a club, make every effort not to be a social failure, or merely drift with the tide. There is no aim here.

What if a captain set out to sea in a ship that had no rudder and could not be navigated? What if the captain did not know just where he was going? What if he had no destination, no reason for going out to sea and then pointing the nose of his vessel into harbor?

The ship must know its way in order to arrive. It must know the port ahead long before it leaves the port behind.

The crippled girl knew it when she saw herself healed. The hunchback knew it when he hung from that bar in the gym. And the businessman knew it when he crowded his small office with customers.

Decide on a goal.

Take aim with your mind.
Wait on direction.
Then watch the miracle happen.
Your forces will help you achieve it!

Chapter **9**

Wherefore lift up the hands which hang down, and the feeble knees; . . .

Hebrews 12:12

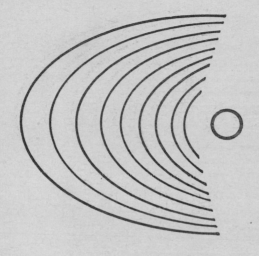

How can you explain that sudden impulse, that warning tap on the shoulder that prompted you to step aside and miss that fatal bullet?

What woke you in the middle of the night in order to extinguish the cigarette that was setting your mattress on fire?

What made you jump up from the breakfast table without any reason, go to the window, and then rush out in the nick of time to rescue your small son, floating face down in the swimming pool?

The story is told of a New York policeman coming off duty at a late hour. He was walking along Fourteenth Street, when suddenly someone behind him gave him a hard push.

The officer was all too familiar with the tactics of muggers—they had attacked him more than once. This time he decided to return the hard blow with a thrust of his own hard fist.

He wheeled around to meet his assailant. There was nobody there.

The sidewalk was deserted. He walked ahead. At that instant, a section of cornice fell from one of the old buildings. It struck the sidewalk, inches away from where he had been standing. If he had not wheeled around, if he had not moved when he did, the iron missile would have struck and killed him.

When he reached the station house, he reported the incident in all its gruesome detail. It was then that a fellow officer related how a "hunch" had tapped him on the shoulder only the day before. He had had the urge to stoop down and tie his open shoelace. The gesture saved his life from a missile that fell in his path, aimed at him by some juvenile delinquents, taunting him from a roof.

How many times have you experienced a sudden, unexplainable urge to proceed or retreat while on a journey either by car or on foot?

An incident which comes to mind is that of a neighbor's boy who was coming home from school one wintry day. It was late. All the light had gone from the sky.

As usual, the boy was about to take the familiar shortcut—up and down the hill, across the pond, and around the bend. He had to climb a fence on the last lap of his homecoming and go across the thick ice—just as he had yesterday and the day before.

But somehow when he reached the fence, a warning voice within him told him not to climb over and take the usual trip across the pond.

It was not until morning that he learned how important it had been to him to obey the silent precaution. The ice, his father told him, had melted, and he would have drowned in the deep waters, with only darkness to view his demise.

No doubt you have had instances in which your life was in danger, and you found yourself dangling at the end of the proverbial rope. Then came the flash—that inner urge compelling you to action. Good thing you listened, emerging somewhat shaken but safe and sound, snatched as it were from the jaws of certain death.

Do you recall the night you telephoned that

despondent cousin of yours who was about to end her life? Your words proved a calming influence. But what prompted your call? You do not know, except to say it was a hunch. Yet what was it primed the summons?

What woke you up in the middle of the night with the perfect solution to a pressing problem—the words to the song you were writing—the order to lock the back door or to open it for the dog?

What made you dash out to the kitchen in the nick of time and snatch the bottle of bleach out of your baby's fingers?

What made a teacher take school discipline into her own hands, incurring the displeasure of the school principal, until he learned that her hunch had saved thirty lives?

Miss Ames, a third-grade teacher, stopped in the middle of an arithmetic problem to order her class to its feet. She marched them out of the door and herded them out to the playground.

There was ice on the playground. It was winter. It was snowing hard, and the children were cold and uncomfortable.

The principal happened to look out of the window and the sight of the shivering children was too much for him. He sent his secretary to summon Miss Ames to the office to explain her uncalled-for conduct. She was on her way when he heard the crash—the fall of the heavy ceiling which crushed thirty chairs and desks. It might have crushed the children, too. She had evacuated them as if at a signal.

What prompted the premonition? Miss Ames was a listener. She did not silence the still, small voice that had spoken its warning. It had taken courage to dismiss the class without first getting orders from the front office. But it was that courage that had saved thirty small lives.

What was the secret behind the seeming miracle?

How did it work?

In this particular case, the clue lay in the inner prompting which Miss Ames obeyed without question.

She heard the voice.

She did not question.

She did not argue.

She caught the prompting.

She took action.

Have you ever sat back in your seat at the theatre and wondered how it came about that the performance before your eyes proceeds without a hitch? After all, the actors are human. The orchestra is made up of men at their instruments. The singers have arms and legs and torsos, just like you, as well as memory banks which fail them at times, just as they fail you and me.

But they speak their lines without making

any errors. They play the music without pause. They sing their songs with every note, every word in place.

Who and what is responsible?

You may not be aware of it—not many know of its existence. But all of this perfection emerges from a prompter's box, a little tiny box set out of sight under the stage. All of this perfection is due to a man who sits in that little box under the stage, screened from view. Yet, it is the prompter who picks up the beat of the music before the performance begins. It is the prompter who gives the performers their cues. It is the prompter who whispers the words in the play when the actors forget their lines. If the prompter fails, the performance fails.

So it is within the mind of man. You must listen to that prompting within you. It is this that primes your pump.

Listen! Always listen!

Listening is a requisite when you utilize the power that is inherent in mental telepathy, particularly when you are in the process of communicating with yourself. Listening is equally essential when you set up a communication system with another.

The case of John Morley is an interesting one. John was a firm believer in mental telepathy. He induced his fiancée to act as a receiving set. Here is a good example of trial and error.

John arranged to communicate with Evelyn every day at noon sharp.

This was the time both took their lunch hour. Of course they worked miles apart.

At first John sent Evelyn a single word in the hope she would be able to receive it. Each evening they would check to ascertain the results.

It took a week of practice to prove to both of them that he would made the better receiver of the two and Evelyn the better sending instrument.

Now each day, it was Evelyn who sent a message to John and John who tuned in.

It took a week of dedicated experimenting to achieve success. But this success expanded from a single word into a sentence and finally a lengthy communication that required no visible wires.

Of course they were delighted with these results. They went beyond their initial efforts and put their findings to good use in many areas of their lives.

They began using mental telepathy to send each other words of encouragement, requests to fulfill, things to remember and warnings in times of danger.

Their method was simple.

They chose a time decided upon between

them—focusing on the picture of each other until the face was clear. Then Evelyn concentrated. The thought was fixed, each word in place. It was only then that she sent it to John. As Evelyn explained it, her words flew out from her like birds on the wing. She always experienced the sensation of her work as having been accomplished. The message had been sent. It had been received at the other end.

The whole operation took less than a minute. At times, it was a matter of seconds with Evelyn, functioning as a radio-sending station, sending John the message which was picked up by his subconscious mind, functioning as a receiving station.

Yes. You can speak to people. You can cure them, help them, warn them, without so much as uttering an audible word.

Don't be discouraged if it doesn't work the first time you try it.

When you first studied arithmetic, your problems did not always work out correctly, did they? Yet you did not doubt the principle of mathematics. You knew that the fault lay with you. The power is there. It can do anything provided you apply the right principle.

If things go wrong in the beginning, don't lose faith and give up. This is what often happens and why so many people fail. Hold on. Just because you turn off your radio does not mean that the program is not on. The forces stand ready to help you. They are always there. Try tuning in again.

But in order to make it a part of your life, you must encourage it to manifest.

You must entrust yourself to a conviction just as a swimmer trusts himself to the water. In order to swim you must know that the sea will keep you afloat. You must give yourself over to the sea, or sink because you persist in struggling.

The courage to float, to launch forth, is often accompanied by an urge or hunch to take action in some direction. Something tells you to act at once, to take a step with no questions, no equivocation—even if ridicule seems to assail you.

At times, the courage of your conviction may attract the scorn of your friends and neighbors. "What made you do it?" they demand of you.

What is the answer?

This is shrouded in mystery. But it is there as plain as your hand in front of your face, attesting to the reality of its working power.

No doubt, you have had the experience upon leaving your house of being seized by a feeling of uneasiness. Something seems to warn you not to close the door. Why? What's wrong? You walk back into the kitchen. There, on the table are your house keys where you had left them. If you had closed the door you would have locked yourself out.

The important thing to remember is to apply your faith in operating your experiments in mental telepathy.

Do you wish to communicate with someone?

Do you wish some special message yourself?

Just remember it's possible. Mental telepathy is always at work!

Chapter 10

Then shall the lame man leap as a hart, and the tongue of the dumb sing: for in the wilderness shall waters break out, and streams in the desert.

Isaiah 35:6

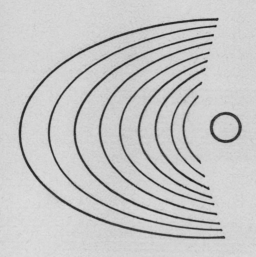

Catholic? Protestant? Jew? Agnostic? Atheist? What is your belief?

Do you favor the efficacy of personal prayer? Perhaps priestly intercession or ritual are your means of guidance. You may reject any notion of Deity and still practice a method of your own.

Scientific research has demonstrated that basic laws exist governing the mental process of your mind. There is a principle which is present in all religions. There is an underlying pattern in all faiths, even those that practice the dark art of voodoo.

Primitive cultures still abound all over the world. They exist in Haiti as well as such remote regions as the island of Yap. It is here that the witch doctor is in power.

Healthy men have been known to die when he sticks pins into a doll made in the victim's image. Strong men grow weak when the witch doctor points the finger bone of a dead man at them. However, scientific scrutiny of these occurrences has produced some startling revelations. Psychologists have come to the illuminating conclusion that the victims killed themselves by willing themselves to death, placing their faith in the witch doctor's ability to kill them.

Dr. Walter B. Cannon, famous for his pioneering work among the Haitian natives, discovered that those who left voodoo and took up Christianity could remain untouched by the powerful magic of the voodoo priest! Dr. Cannon further learned that faith in voodoo produced not only psychological changes in thinking, but corresponding changes in the body.

The weak grew weaker. The ill grew deathly ill. This change in body chemistry was achieved by the witch doctor who, versed in the art of mental telepathy, used his evil skill on his subjects. On the other hand, he could also turn on his power to bring about positive results should this request, accompanied by proper payment, be made him.

Death by voodoo is an example of what someone else can do to you, provided you are vulnerable to outer suggestion. You can always protect yourself with the shield of your own thought which, like the barriers used in parades by the police department, reads:

DO NOT CROSS
THESE LINES

Perhaps you are asking yourself if it was the power of God inculcated in the witch doctor that killed his victim. *No.*

Was it the power within the witch doctor? *No.*

Well, where was the power? Just where power is always present—within the human being involved in the case. The power is always within you. It is never outside of you.

Nothing can touch you unless you admit it freely or in an unguarded moment. This is why it is important to obey the admonition to always stand guard at the door of your mind.

It is your conscious mind which first receives the impression. That impression takes action. It steps down into your subconscious mind. It is here that the workshop of miracles takes place. This requires emotion as its fuel.

Remember that your subconscious mind will act *only* upon instructions fired by your emotions. These must be accompanied by feeling. It is feeling that produces either fear or faith. Emotion is always the governing factor.

This is why religion plays such an important role in mental and spiritual healing. Religious emotion is a powerful agent. It is adept at conveying suggestions to the subconscious. Deep emotion is a powerful factor in arousing the subconscious forces to take action.

The Old Testament records innumerable incidents of healing.

When the people of Israel marched through the wilderness, they came into a land infested by snakes. Many were bitten. Of course, like all primitive people, they attributed every calamity to an angry God.

But Moses was wise. He fashioned a huge serpent of brass and placed it on a high pole so that the entire camp could see it. The victims are said to have recovered, proving that suggestion always operates upon the subconscious.

It is important that you convince your subconscious mind that you believe in it. Believe you will receive that which you ask. Instruct your subconscious mind to act on that belief, presenting to you definite plans for obtaining your desire.

But you must be honest with yourself. You cannot pray for sunshine and negate your faith by carrying an umbrella!

A wise king once expressed it succinctly when he said that to be ambitious for wealth and yet always expecting to be poor—to be always doubting your ability to get what you long for—is like trying to reach East by traveling West. There is no philosophy which will help a man to succeed when he is always doubting his ability to do so and thus attracting failure.

You get a mental picture. You hold that mental picture. It is recorded. It is broadcast —both within and without. While it lies like a fetus within your being, it produces action— physical action. Simultaneously, outside of you, it tends to attract the materializing units.

This is the emergence, the birth.

Of course, it is not enough simply to make the mental picture in your success formula. You must add the ingredients of expectancy and faith. These screen out pictures of fear, doubt, and failure. They channel the main thought to the organs of response.

They make straight the way.

They result in action.

Chapter 11

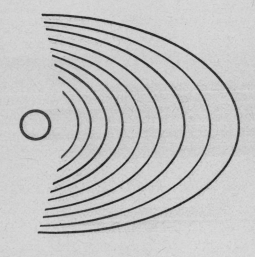

In my Father's house are many man-
sions: if it were not so, I would have told
you. I go to prepare a place for you.

John 14:2

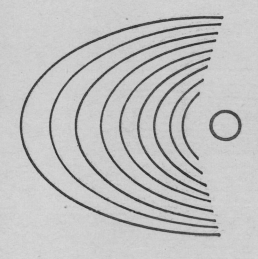

The story is told of a young singer who was
called to Hollywood for an audition. She went
to the airport to arrange her flight.

Her money had already found its way into
the hands of the clerk behind the counter, and
he was in the process of assigning her a seat
number, when a sudden impulse seized her to
cancel the trip. She heard the voice clearly,

commanding her to obey. She tried to shut it out, but it called even louder:

"Cancel the trip! Cancel the trip!"

She decided to obey. Without a word of explanation, she reached for her check and dashed off, claiming her luggage on the way.

The ride home in the taxi left her shaken. She could not sleep that night, demanding to know why she had cancelled her flight and lost the opportunity of a lifetime by not reporting for the audition that her agent had gone to great trouble to arrange. What plausible excuse would she be able to offer him when he telephoned the next day to berate her for her failure to report to the producer? Here she was, losing a golden opportunity to make stardom.

All night long she tossed and turned in her bed. She blamed herself for having been so foolish as to listen to her intuition. A woman's intuition, she argued, was never to be trusted. Why had she listened to that voice? Where did that voice come from? Why had she felt compelled to obey?

The next day, the answer came. It shouted from the first page of the morning paper the boy left at her door.

The plane she had been scheduled to take had crashed en route with every life lost—as hers would have been if she had not been respectful to that still, small voice within her.

Just so, there is within you a mighty force which can reach out into the future and protect you in the present. Within you is that Mind of yours—a mind that is all-wise, all-powerful, a mind that is entirely apart from the mind that you consciously use in your everyday affairs, yet which is one with the Universal Mind.

Your subconscious mind partakes of this wisdom and power, and it is through your subconscious that you can draw upon it in times of warning, just as it flashes to others.

Always remember that the Universal Mind is omnipotent. And since the subconscious mind is part of the Universal Mind, there is no limit to the things which it can do when it is given the power to act.

The power of the subconscious is unlimited. Whatever is necessary for you will be done. It will give you the strength and the ability to do the impossible. It will bring you whatever you need. The Gospels state:

> *The Kingdom of Heaven is within you.*

This does not mean the acquisition of material things only. It turns every spoke of the wheel, including that of danger.

You have heard of people who have seen death staring them in the face. There seemed

nothing they could do. Things went black.
They lost consciousness. When they recovered,
they found that the danger had passed. In the
moment of need, their subconscious mind
pushed the conscious out of the way while it
met and overcame the danger. Yet, they themselves, could do nothing to help themselves.

Man lives and moves and has his being in
this great subconscious mind. It supplies the
intuition that so often carries a woman straight
to a point that may require hours of cumber-
some reasoning in a man.

Perhaps, at times, the man of the family
may laugh at a woman because she has a
hunch they should do something or go somewhere and no logical explanation for the so-
called silly suggestion that is tapping her on
the shoulder.

Follow your hunch!

Neither explain yourself nor excuse it. Don't
permit yourself to be beaten back or have
your suggestion analyzed.

An analysis of a negative will never produce the synthesis of a positive.

If you have a hunch—a strong urge to do
something—do it! Don't discuss it. When you
talk about your business—you give it away.
Keep your own counsel until you have achieved
your objective.

Here is an example of how mental telepathy
was used to decided advantage when it was

applied by a young and somewhat fearful secretary. It had its inception in the office of a prosperous, yet stodgy stockbroker.

It seemed that her employer was reluctant to give her a raise. Her work was good but it went unrewarded. Her accuracy was taken for granted. As a matter of fact, so was she. The stockbroker regarded her as just another office machine.

Then she decided she wanted to change the pattern.

She began to practice the simple skill of utilizing mental telepathy on the unhappy working conditions that prevailed. She determined that she was being paid much too little. So she began to project thought forms of the increase she wanted. She saw her employer more kindly, more receptive, more appreciative. She got to work creating the new pattern.

Every day at lunch she ate very hurriedly in order to have half of the hour left to talk to her boss—mentally. She would go to his office while he was out for his lunch and sit in her chair that faced the one he used when he gave her dictation.

She could see him seated there, smiling and attentive—nothing like the picture he actually made of a sullen, withdrawn entity. She even dressed him in a modish suit with a bright tie to match.

Each day—for two weeks—the dialogue proceeded, loud and clear, never changing. Her argument was always the same.

"I deserve a raise."

"You will give me my raise."

"You will say 'thank you' when I stay over-time."

"You will be grateful to me when you find all those letters on your desk in the morning, the ones you dictated long after hours, finished and waiting on your signature."

"You will give me my raise."

"You will give me at least ten dollars more a week."

"In fact you will give me a bonus!"

"Yes. You will act on these suggestions!"

Then she visualized herself, standing in front of him and receiving the raise she requested. She even saw herself thanking him.

The weeks went by, and nothing happened.

It was time to become discouraged. But she continued her mental projection. You see, she believed in the value of using mental telepathy as an aid in achieving her promotion.

One day, the boss called her into his office.

She went in with her pad, thinking he was going to give her the usual stream of dictation.

Instead, he said, "I don't know why I'm sending for you. It's not to give you dicta-tion. And I don't know why I'm doing this. But I feel you deserve a raise. How about ten dollars now and a five-hundred-dollar bonus at Christmas?"

What's more, he discovered that his secretary was very pretty besides being very efficient, and their relationship took a radical turn for the better.

Now, in your case, it may take time to test your skill. You may not succeed in achieving a raise or the richer reward of recognition. You may not even reach your goal.

Don't be afraid to fail!

But don't entertain a thought of failure. If you do, you are already a failure!

Many years ago a certain young man ran for the legislature in Illinois. He was badly beaten. He went into business. He failed. He spent more than fifteen years paying off the debts of a partner who cheated him. He met a girl and fell in love. They were engaged to be married. His fiancée died. He ran for Congress. He was beaten. He could not obtain an appointment with the U.S. Land Office. He tried turning his efforts toward a possible candidacy in the Senate. Again he failed.

Now what lay ahead of him? Failure and still more failure?

No.

He had a mental concept of himself. He was determined to succeed. And in the end, he rose to the heights of being elected to the most coveted post in the country.

Perhaps you have already guessed his name, the name of that very great president, Abraham Lincoln, whose record of failure is a golden example of what the indomitable spirit in man can achieve.

Perhaps you, too, are a dreamer who has met with defeat all your life.

Yet your time will come.

If you take the proven steps, a whole new universe will unfold in front of you. Your use of mental telepathy will serve you in every department of your efforts.

But you have to have faith. You have to believe. That is the fuel in the engine. Belief connects the switch in your hand with the power that turns on the motor!

Chapter 12

I have fought a good fight, I have fin-ished my course, I have kept the faith: . . .

2 Timothy 4:7

Mental telepathy may be induced by pre-ceding your session with a meditation.

Take some deep breaths.

Repeat a familiar prayer.

You might even have some soft music play-ing to help you set your mood.

Light a candle or two. This aids in creating a receptive attitude.

121

Lozanov's method?

Now take time to give thanks for everything in your world. Bless all who come to mind.

Take another breath or two, softly, as if you had an ashtray full of ashes under your nose which you were careful not to disturb. Breathing must be a relaxed measure for it is not only power being sent to your lungs but to your every cell that hungers for the food in the air.

Now relax.

②→ Now take action and voice your request.

Do you wish to communicate with someone?

Do you want something special for yourself—some deep desire to be granted—some information about a person, a place, a decision—some reference to an action in the past that you have taken in order to proceed in a certain matter, such as a return of memory to find a lost object, a name that has slipped from your mind, an address, a dredging up of some event in the past, or some definite pointers of guidance for your future?

XXXX Mental telepathy is always at work! ← X

The action of thought creates a thought form which projects itself into space without regard for time. Ideas that give rise to things are in a universal HERE and an ever-present NOW!

Know with conviction that nothing is impossible.

The power within you is limitless. It is the

inexhaustible source of everything you may require for the highest development and the greatest accomplishment in your life. Whatever you direct the power within you to produce will invariably be produced, provided you apply the right principle.

There is within you an irresistible force enabling you to succeed in undertakings that would stagger your imagination.

It is your mind—a mind that is all-wise, all-powerful, and all-loving—that works in all things. Call on it to serve you. Praise it when it serves you. Harness it in every department of your life. There is no big or little in God. A sparrow is as meaningful as an elephant. There is no big or little in you. It is all part of the great whole. *UNIVERSAL MIND.*

Whatever your creed, the important thing to remember is that you need to return to the inner center of yourself. It is here that mental telepathy acts as a spiritual force for good.

The story is told that God sought to secrete the human soul where man was least likely to look. That is why He placed it deep within the human being—like an altar in the heart of a church.

The secret of answered prayer is to reach that center. Once you touch it, you establish rapport between yourself and your power.

That is why prayer is necessary.

Keep on praying, and, in your prayer

explanation of
in prayer
in ①   *2ᵉ partie du Notre Père et de*
Je vous salue Marie.

moments, see yourself safe and secure. See safety and security for the loved ones around you. Now embrace the whole world, stranger and enemy too.

Now prove your prayer by reaching out in thought to everything everywhere—praising, blessing, acknowledging, harmonizing, loving, giving as well as receiving—for here is the highest form—and the shortest path to achieving mental telepathy!